The
Great Western
Broad Gauge

LAURENCE WATERS

Ian Allan
PUBLISHING

Contents

Front cover: A down mail service hauled by an unidentified 'Rover' class 4-2-2 picks up mail at speed near Cullompton on 6 May 1891. The postman watches carefully over the scene. The pattern of the mailbag apparatus is very similar to the one installed at Didcot railway centre. *From an original painting by George Heiron based on a photograph taken by Rev A. H. Malan/GWT Collection*

Back cover, top: The last broad gauge through service to Penzance, the 10.15am 'Cornishman' hauled by 'Rover' class 4-2-2 *Great Western* stands at Paddington on 20 May 1892. The very last broad gauge passenger train the service to Plymouth departed at 5pm on the same day behind fellow class member *Bulkeley*. *GWT Collection*

Back cover, bottom: This well known picture shows a line of 11 'Rover' class 4-2-2s. In the foreground is the engine *Sebastopol. GWT Collection*

Half title: An up broad gauge service speeds past milepost 309½ in around 1891. Although the location has not been noted by the photographer, the mileage, which is measured via Bristol, indicates the location as the Redruth area. The engine is an ex-South devon Railway 4-4-0ST with open driving splashers and is either No 2130 *Lance* or No 2131 *Osiris*. These engines were built by the SDR in 1875 and were the only two to feature this design. Both were withdrawn in May 1875. Notice also that the mixed gauge track has been laid using chairs and sleepers. *GWT Collection*

Title page: Sultan stands in the yard at Westbourne Park in 1873. Built at Swindon in November 1847, it was the last of six engines that formed the 'second lot passenger class'. It is seen here with a spectacle plate and an express passenger tender. Note that the brake gear has been painted in a light colour and the tender has reversed-corner lining. *Sultan* ceased work in June 1874 with a final mileage recorded as 727,300. It was replaced by a new engine in September 1876. Interestingly, *Sultan* was the engine used in Frith's famous painting of Paddington station. *GWT Collection*

First published 1999

ISBN 0 7110 2634 3

© Ian Allan Publishing Ltd 1999

Published by Ian Allan Publishing

an imprint of Ian Allan Publishing Ltd, Terminal House, Shepperton, Surrey TW17 8AS.
Printed by Ian Allan Printing Ltd, Riverdene Business Park, Hersham, Surrey KT12 4RG.

Code: 9902/B

As a Great Western enthusiast I have always been fascinated by the broad gauge and although pictures tell some of the story, it was not until the Taunton Group of the Great Western Society installed the broad-gauge track at Didcot Railway Centre that I was able to appreciate just how wide this gauge was. In 1986, the replica *Iron Duke* came to Didcot and was operated for the first time on genuine broad-gauge track. It looked magnificent, and I can remember standing watching her run and trying to imagine this magnificent class of engine speeding through Didcot all those years ago.

It has been said that the broad gauge was an anachronism and probably should not have been built — but imagine if this gauge had been adopted throughout the country: the comfort, the extra carrying capacity for both goods and passengers, and, above all, the ability to run fast with the extra stability and safety that a wider gauge would offer. If only.

The Photographs

In preparing this book, it has been a pleasant surprise to find just how many photographs of broad-gauge locomotives have survived. The photographs in the book date from around 1850 up to the removal of the broad gauge in May 1892. Some of these early photographs are remarkable, for in this age of fast emulsions and automatic cameras,

it must be remembered that photographers had to make their own plates, prior to the invention of the gelatin dry plate process by Maddox in 1871, and for some years after.

The first practical photographic process, the daguerreotype, was invented by Frenchman Louis Daguerre in about 1835, the same year that the Great Western Railway was formed. The negative-positive process that is used today was the work of Henry Fox-Talbot. The Calotype-type (later Talbotype) was introduced in around 1841, the year that the Great Western main line to Bristol was opened. Neither of these early processes would have been very practical for railway photography. Talbot's early experiments used paper negatives, although the later Talbotype process used glass as a base and could have been used for some earliest shots.

Many of the photographs in this book were almost certainly taken using Scott-Archer's wet collodion process. This was invented in 1851, and

Below: A view of Southall, looking west in mixed-gauge days. Notice, however, the broad-gauge-only crossing. The station was rebuilt after the quadrupling of the lines in 1877/8. Southall was for many years the junction station for the Brentford branch. This broad-gauge branch opened for goods on 18 July 1859 and for passenger services on 1 May 1850, the broad gauge being removed in March 1876. Passenger services were withdrawn on 4 May 1942, but part of the branch remains open for freight traffic. *GWT Collection*

superseded Talbot's process. Glass plates were coated in situ by the photographer using a dark-tent and exposed in the camera when wet, only being dried after development. Within a few years of Richard Leach Maddox inventing the gelatin dry plate process in 1871, photographers were able to buy boxed glass plates. For the first time, plates were fast enough to capture moving objects.

During these early years of photography, there was no film speed as we know it — exposure was by trial and error, using a tripod for every shot. If it could be measured, some of these early emulsions probably had an effective film speed of no more than 1 or 2 ISO (ASA). Hence there were many static shots. The moving train pictures of the 1880s and 1890s are remarkable for the time, but probably owe much to the angle of the shot (three-quarters front), the use of wide aperture lenses (first produced by Josef Petzval in 1840) and the skill of the photographer rather than fast emulsion speeds.

Below: 'Fire Fly' class *Actaeon*, built by Nasmyth, Gaskell & Co, and pictured here at Gloucester on 15 March 1857. The engine had a rather chequered career: delivered in December 1841, it was driven by Gooch to and from Exeter on the opening of through services on 1 May 1844. In June 1850 it was in steam at Swansea and used for the opening of the South Wales Railway. *Actaeon* suffered a severe boiler explosion at Gloucester on 7 February 1855, but was subsequently rebuilt at Swindon in August 1856 with a domeless boiler. The engine ceased work in March 1868 but was used as a stationary boiler at Newport until its final withdrawal in July 1870. *GWT Collection*

A number of the photographs in this book are the work of the Rev A. H. Mallan who mainly operated around Bristol and the West of England. W. T. Good, who lived at Carlton Terrace, Westbourne Park, photographed in the Westbourne Park and Paddington areas, and a number of the Swindon pictures were the work of Mr Prothero, a local photographer.

Acknowledgements

I would like to thank the following for their help in preparing this book: Bill Peto, Mike Jolly, Peter Webber, Phil Kelley, Peter Treloar, John Mosse, the Fire Fly Trust, the Great Western Society, the Great Western Trust, the Ian Allan Library and the Broad Gauge Society.

Special thanks to Dr Rosemary Painter for proof reading the manuscript.

There have been several excellent books written on the broad gauge, but the best for the locomotive historian is the RCTS publication *Locomotives of the Great Western Railway, Part 2: Broad Gauge.*

For those who are interested in studying the subject further, I can recommend the excellent Broad Gauge Society, details of which can be obtained from the Honorary Secretary, Alan Garner, 8 Finches Park Road, Lindfield, Haywards Heath, West Sussex RH16 2DN.

Laurence Waters
Oxford
October 1998

CHAPTER 1

The Great Western Broad Gauge

The first proposal for a railway between London and Bristol probably came in 1824 from the London & Bristol Rail Road Company. Like many others at the time, this proved to be over-ambitious and costly, and it soon passed into history.

In August 1832, four Bristol businessmen resurrected the idea of a Bristol to London railway. Further meetings were held, and in January 1833 the committee, which by now numbered 15, agreed to provide the funds for a preliminary survey and to appoint an engineer. On 7 March 1833, the company made what was arguably its most important decision, by appointing the 27-year-old engineer to the Bristol Dock Company and designer of the Clifton Suspension Bridge, Isambard Kingdom Brunel. After a rather rapid survey, which was completed in June, Brunel put the cost of construction at £2,800,000. His report was

Above: No book on the broad gauge would be complete if it did not include Frith's famous painting of Paddington station in 1862. Apart from the detail of the station and the passengers and staff, it also shows a typical broad-gauge train of the period.
GWT Collection

accepted on 30 July 1833 at the meeting in Bristol, and this resolution was passed:

'A company should be formed for the establishment of railway communications between Bristol and London, and for that purpose a body of directors for Bristol be appointed, who, in conjunction with a similar body to be appointed in London, shall constitute a general board of management for securing subscriptions and obtaining an Act of Parliament for effecting the same object.'

Left: A lithograph of the interior of the first engine shed at Paddington. Constructed by the Great Western Company and opened in around March or May 1838, it comprised a central 130ft diameter roundhouse with a pair of straight sheds tagged on to each end. The whole complex measured about 360ft x 80ft. The roundhouse contained a 35ft turntable and eight radial roads. The shed was closed and removed in March 1852 and replaced by a much larger depot that opened during the same month at Westbourne Park. The two identifiable engines on the lithograph are *Elephant* and *Rover*, which were too big for the turntable and had to be separated from their tenders to be turned: note the tender being turned in the picture. *G. Measom/GWT Collection*

Lower left: A view of the 'one-sided' station at Slough, dated 1841. Brunel built this design of station at locations such as Taunton, Exeter, Gloucester and Reading where the town was generally situated on one side of the railway. In the background is the station hotel, and in the right foreground is the goods shed office roof. *GWT Collection*

Below right: An early drawing depicting New Swindon in 1847, viewed from the junction of the Gloucester and Great Western lines. The engine depicted is 'Fire Fly' class *Fire Brand*. On the right is the first engine shed and some early signals towering over the policeman's hut. On the left is the railway village. *GWT Collection*

On 19 August 1833, the newly formed Bristol & London Committee adopted the name 'Great Western Railway'. The prospectus offered potential subscribers the chance to invest in the new company at a cost of £100 per share with the intention of raising the £3,000,000 required to construct the line.

The first Parliamentary bill was deposited in November 1833, but, due to a lack of funds, was only for the sections between London and Reading and Bristol and Bath, with the 70-mile centre section between Reading and Bath only to be completed as and when the money was raised. After many objections and a number of changes, the bill passed its second reading in the House of Commons on 10 March 1834. Unfortunately, on 25 July it was rejected by the House of Lords, on the grounds that the bill 'offered no security for the completion of the whole line between London and Bristol'.

Unperturbed by this, the company issued another prospectus in November 1834 for completion of the whole route. This time they were more successful, and on 27 February 1835 the bill had a successful second reading. Its third reading on 28 August was also successful and on 31 August 1835 the bill received its Royal Assent. The Great Western Railway was born. Soon after work had started, Brunel proclaimed: 'The railway is now in progress. I am thus engineer to the finest work in England. A handsome salary, on excellent terms with my directors, and all going smoothly.'

Interestingly, the omission by the company of a gauge clause from the Act allowed Brunel to consider the railway's track gauge. He had always advocated that a wide gauge would allow high speeds with exceptional stability, and in a report to the company on 15 September 1835, Brunel proposed a gauge width of between 6ft 10in and 7ft 0in, 'which would, I think admit of sufficient width of carriages for all purposes'. The gauge adopted was 7ft 0in, later changed to 7ft 0¼in (2,140mm) to ease clearance.

Brunel's reasoning was that the wider gauge allowed the boilers of the engines to be placed within the frames, rather than on top as in the narrow gauge, thus offering greater stability at speed. The same reasoning also applied to carriages and wagons. One of the main obstacles to using the wider gauge was removed, when, owing to a disagreement with the London & Birmingham Railway over land rights, the proposal for the railway to terminate at Euston station was abandoned. Instead it was decided to terminate the line on land adjacent to the Paddington Canal.

When the Great Western opened its line from Paddington to Maidenhead on 4 June 1838, the company provided eight passenger services each weekday and six on Sundays. On 2 June 1838, the *Sun* newspaper (not related to today's paper) reported:

'The first portion of this stupendous and important undertaking having been completed to Maidenhead — a distance of 24 miles by railway and 27 miles by road — an experimental trip was held yesterday — Thursday — made by directors and a large party of friends. This railway may well claim for itself the title of "Great", for it throws completely into the shade all of those lines already opened, whether we regard the magnitude of the scale on which the arrangements have been made, the speed and power of the engines provided or the extent of the traffic it contemplates from the immediate connection between its Bristol terminus and the United States of America. There are four descriptions of carriages, all of which are about 12ft in height from the rails to the top. The extra first-class reminds us more of one of the comfortable state cabins of one of our first-class river steamers than anything else we can liken it to. It is filled along the sides with large plate glass windows commanding a most extensive view of the surrounding country, and will accommodate from 18 to 20 persons. The engines to draw these immense moving houses are of corresponding size and power, and with their tenders weigh upwards of 20 tons each.'

By December 1838 the number of trains had increased to nine, with four short trains serving the intermediate stations between Paddington and Drayton.

At this time the permanent way was causing problems, giving a firm and uncomfortable ride. Brunel's method of using piles to anchor the track proved to be the problem. Engineer Nicholas Wood's report dated December 1838 states 'the mode adopted in laying the rails is, I think, attempting to do that in a difficult and expensive manner, which may be done at least as well in a simple and more economical manner — that the piles do not contribute to the firmness of base of the railway; their action seems to prevent the contact of timbers with the ground.' The board adopted the report with the result that piles were not used again, the scantling of the longitudinal timbers was increased and a heavier rail was used.

Locomotive Department returns for the six months ending June 1849 show passenger miles run 82,730, goods and ballast 13,722, and mineral

3,900. Salaries and wages totalled £2,943 17s 3d and materials such as coke, oil, tallow, waste, gas, water and engine parts came to a further £2,706 9s 8d.

In July 1839 the line was opened to Twyford, and the year's returns show 606,396 passengers carried; by March 1840 when the railway was opened through to Reading, this had risen to over one million. Trains usually consisted of three open second-class carriages (216 passengers) and three firsts (96 passengers). At this time 'persons from the lower station in life' (ordinary working folk) were carried on the evening mixed goods in open trucks which were usually placed next to the engine. 'The goods train passengers will be conveyed in uncovered trucks by the goods train only, and 14lb of luggage allowed for each.' It was to take Gladstone's Railway Regulation Act of November 1844 to stop the practice: the Act provided for seats and proper covered accommodation for the passengers, at least one stopping train daily in each direction at a speed of not less than 12mph including stops, and a charge of one penny a mile. These were known as Parliamentary or 'cheap' trains, and the company initially constructed eight third-class coaches for the service. It could be said that the company complied reluctantly, as the first cheap trains, the 7am service from Paddington to Bristol and the 9.30am Bristol to Paddington, both had journey times of about 9¼hr.

The 1842 timetable shows seven through trains each day to Bristol. Through services between Paddington and Exeter were introduced during May 1844, and these opened with eight Down and seven Up trains, each taking on average some 7½hr to reach their destination. During 1845, the Great

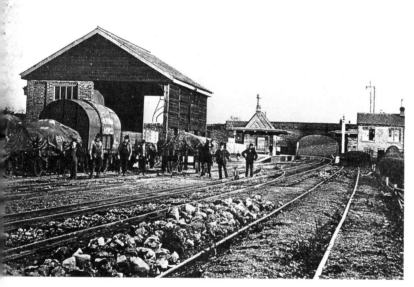

Left: A view of Wootton Bassett in mixed-gauge days. A temporary station some three miles to the west of the town at Hay Lane (Wootton Bassett Road) had been opened on 17 December 1840. The new station at Wootton Bassett, which was much nearer to the town and is seen here, was opened in September 1841. The line was converted to mixed gauge in June 1874. Notice the broad-gauge and narrow-gauge goods vehicles, together with the station shunting horse in the goods-shed siding and the early-type signalbox at right angles to the line. *GWT Collection*

Below: Chippenham station in 1841. The short platforms reflect the length of the trains at this time. The large building on the left is the goods shed. *GWT Collection*

Above: The western terminus of the line was at Bristol (Temple Meads), seen here in this rather fine drawing by Bourne. At this time the shed was probably shunted by using either man power or horse. The train shed was used as a car park for a number of years, and although still devoid of tracks has now been restored to something of its former glory. *Ian Allan Library*

Western speeded up the Exeter services with the running time to Exeter reduced to just 4¼ hr. This included the compulsory 10min refreshment stop at Swindon, a rather inconvenient arrangement agreed in 1841 between the company and J. & C. Rigby.

The Rigbys agreed to build Swindon's station and other buildings at their own expense, if the company agreed to stop all regular passenger trains 'for a reasonable period of about ten minutes', and also agreed that no other stopping place for refreshments should be provided between London and Bristol. The money the company saved was spent in the end, but the stop was certainly not inconvenient for the passengers as there were no lavatories provided in trains at this time. Over the years, the lease changed hands for considerable amounts of money, and the problem was not resolved until the Great Western bought the surrender of the lease for about £100,000 on 12 November 1895.

On 4 October 1847, and with safety in mind, the Great Western introduced travelling porters, initially on express trains, but later on all long-distance services. The porter sat facing the carriages in what became known as an 'Iron Coffin' seat, situated at the rear of the locomotive's tender. The job is described thus:

'The business of the Travelling Porter is to ride on the seat placed for him on the tender, and to keep a steady and vigilant look-out along the side and top of the train, so that in the case of an accident to any of the carriages or of any signal from the guard, or any apparently sufficient cause that may come to his observation, he may at once communicate with the engine man, and if necessary stop the train.'

At this time luggage was also carried on the roofs of trains, so he also had to keep an eye on this and stop the train if any fell off or caught fire from sparks from the engine. He was also responsible for checking the carriages, including lights and axleboxes. He did all this for just 25s a week — an arduous job, particularly in bad weather. In 1864 the travelling porter was replaced by a communication cord that ran from the front van to a large gong attached to the front of the tender. The Bristol & Exeter Railway, which was probably more enlightened than the Great Western, did away with travelling porters in 1854, by raising part of the roof in the guard's van and providing a platform seat from where the guard could survey the train.

The Regulation of Railways Act of 1869 compelled railway companies to adopt the cord system of communication on all passenger trains travelling more than 20 miles without stopping.

One of the main virtues of the broad gauge was its stability, and although accidents happened, it was this stability that often kept casualties to a minimum. One of the earliest accidents took place on the evening of 7 September 1841, when, after a bout of severe weather, a landslip occurred at Wootton Bassett, causing the derailment of an Up mail train hauled by 'Star' class 2-2-2 *Rising Star* and 'Fire Fly' class 2-2-2 *Tiger*. Unfortunately, *Tiger* hit the slip and parted company with *Rising Star* which continued unharmed, while *Tiger* together with its

three carriages was derailed. However, once again the stability of the broad gauge saved the day and casualties were light.

The first really serious accident on the Great Western occurred on Christmas Eve 1841, when the 4.30pm Down goods service from Paddington to Bristol hauled by the engine *Hecla*, a 'Leo' class 2-4-0, built by Fenton, Murray & Jackson of Leeds in April 1841, hit a landslip at Sonning. At this time these services carried both goods and third-class passengers (probably in that order of priority). Approximately halfway through Sonning cutting, the train, which consisted of two third-class carriages, a station truck and 17 goods wagons, and was probably travelling at a good speed, ran into the landslip. The sudden stop caused the goods wagons to crush the coaches against *Hecla's* tender. Of the 38 passengers on board, eight were killed and 17 seriously injured; the crash was made all the worse because at this time carriages and wagons were not fitted with spring buffers.

Another serious accident, caused solely by human error, took place on 10 May 1848, when the 12 noon express from Exeter to Paddington, carrying about 200 passengers and hauled by 'Iron Duke' class 4-2-2 *Sultan*, struck at full speed a cattle truck and horse box at Shrivenham station. These two vehicles had apparently been pushed manually onto the main line, without any sort of permission, by a

Above: The Great Western goods shed at Bristol, in another of Bourne's magnificent drawings of the early days of the Great Western. The form of many examples of the earliest goods stock is seen only in Bourne's illustrations. *GWT Collection*

Above right: This lithograph from the *Illustrated London News* of 17 August 1847 supposedly depicts the difficulties in transferring passengers and goods from the broad to the narrow gauge at Gloucester. The lithograph shows the contemporary dress of both railway staff and public, and also the type of luggage carried by passengers at this time. The drawing probably overstates the difficulties of the changeover, but it must have been pretty dire at busy times. *GWT Collection*

couple of porters who were involved in shunting duty in the station yard. The Exeter express of course had right of way, and as no one other than the two porters was aware of the obstruction, *Sultan* together with its train comprising a brake van, three second and three first-class carriages, hit the offending trucks at full speed. The engine and brake van passed by almost unscathed, but the wreckage of the trucks struck the first carriage of the train, killing six passengers and injuring another 13.

Gradually the main-line system was extended. In the southwest, passenger services were inaugurated between Exeter and Plymouth via the South Devon Railway on 2 April 1849, and with the opening of the Royal Albert Bridge at Saltash, were extended via the Cornwall Railway to Truro on 4 May 1859,

and via the West Cornwall Railway to Penzance on 1 March 1867.

The South Wales Railway was incorporated in August 1845 to construct a 143-mile broad-gauge line from Chepstow to Fishguard. The first section of the railway opened for passenger traffic between Chepstow and Swansea on 18 June 1850. The line was worked from the start using Great Western engines and rolling stock, but until the construction of the Wye Bridge in July 1852, the railway was segregated from the rest of the Great Western system. This meant that the engines and rolling stock had to be ferried across the Bristol Channel. The Gooch registers state that in July 1850 some 12 'Fire Fly' locomotives were working passenger services on the railway. Broad-gauge locomotive servicing facilities were initially provided at Chepstow (until August 1854) and also at Swansea, until the removal of the gauge in 1872. Further broad-gauge sheds were opened at Carmarthen Junction in October 1852, at Bullo Pill in August 1854, and during the same month the company opened its main shed and locomotive headquarters at Newport. A small two-road shed was also opened at Cardiff (Newtown) in 1858.

The link with the rest of the system was made with the opening on 19 July 1852 of the 1-mile connection, via Brunel's Wye Bridge, between Chepstow and the Great Western's Chepstow-Grange Court-Gloucester line, thus allowing through services to commence between Paddington and Swansea. The railway was extended from Landore to Carmarthen on 11 October 1852, to Haverfordwest on 2 January 1854 and to New Milford (Neyland) on 15 April 1856. The final section to Fishguard & Goodwick was not opened until 1 July 1899, long after the broad gauge had gone. Engine servicing facilities at New Milford were provided with the re-erection of the old engine shed from Chepstow West.

The third major broad-gauge route, to Birmingham and beyond, began to take shape with the opening of the Oxford Railway branch from Didcot Junction to Oxford on 12 June 1844. The line was extended through to Banbury on 2 September 1850 and to Birmingham on 1 October 1852. As we all know, accidents often happen at the most inconvenient of times. On 30 September 1852, the day before the official opening of the line, a special 10-coach inaugural train containing directors and friends and hauled by the locomotive *Lord of the Isles*, one of Gooch's 'Iron Duke' 4-2-2s, crashed at Aynho into the rear of the preceding mixed train, which was preparing to detach a couple of goods wagons at the station. On hearing the approach of the special, which was running nearly an hour late, the driver of the mixed train, which comprised two passenger carriages and

13

Left: At speed on the footplate of a broad-gauge engine. *GWT Collection*

three goods trucks, tried to move his train away: unfortunately, the rapid start broke the coupling chain between the carriages, leaving the wagons in the path of the rapidly approaching express.

The only brakes on the special train were on the locomotive tender and a second-class coach, so, unable to brake in time, *Lord of the Isles* struck the three wagons, smashing them to pieces. *Lord of the Isles* was derailed but no one was seriously injured. It appears that no one on the special, including Gooch and Brunel, who were on the footplate, knew the road and a disused signal was mistaken for the distant. It seems that, although the line had been doubled, the signalling was still in situ from the time it was just a single-line branch to Banbury. It was obviously 'one of those days' as the engine *Sultan*, another 'Iron Duke' class 4-2-2, which had been sent from Birmingham to render assistance at Aynho, was itself derailed en route.

The new service to Birmingham could hardly be described as rapid. In 1853, the fastest train took 3hr, but in later years this was cut to 2hr 50min. Broad-gauge services were extended through to Wolverhampton on 14 November 1854. Locomotive servicing facilities were opened at Oxford in July 1850, at Birmingham in October 1850 (replaced by Bordesley from 1855) and at Wolverhampton Stafford Road in November 1854.

Unfortunately, despite all of the benefits of the broad gauge, the rest of the country was building its lines to Stephenson's narrow 4ft 8½in gauge,

originating from the coalfields of the northeast. The broad gauge would have been all very well had it been confined to Paddington, Bristol and the southwest, but the Great Western, like other railways, had expanded, and at no less than 10 different locations it encountered the narrow or standard gauge. At these points both goods and passengers had to change trains, and this was all very slow and inconvenient.

Conditions at Gloucester were causing particular problems, with many complaints from both the public and the narrow-gauge companies. Obviously something had to be done, and on 25 June 1845 the government appointed a Gauge Commission to look into the uniformity of gauge. The Great Western from the start was at a disadvantage, for in 1845 there was just 274 miles of broad-gauge track as opposed to 1,901 miles of narrow-gauge track. The commission sat from August until September 1845 and heard many arguments for and against the broad and narrow gauges. Gooch himself was a stalwart of the broad gauge, noting in his diary:

'I had to give evidence on the Bill and had prepared elaborate tables showing the superiority and economy of the broad gauge. We met in a temporary committee room, and the crowd and the heat was excessive. Sitting in this heat all day, and working most of the night in preparing evidence for the witnesses almost broke me down. I shall never forget the passion George Stephenson got into when the decision of the committee was announced. He gave me his mind very freely for fighting the broad gauge against the narrow, in which he said I had been reared. I was not only fighting for my conviction but for my employers, who expressed themselves well satisfied with what I had done.'

Certainly in terms of speed, the broad gauge was at that time unsurpassed. On 11 May 1845, the engine *Great Britain*, one of Gooch's 8ft singles, reportedly reached 74.5mph at Wootton Bassett. This sort of speed was certainly not an isolated occurrence. Even the Bristol & Exeter Railway got in on the act, with one of its 4-2-4 tank engines reportedly reaching 81.8mph down Wellington bank.

Brunel was certainly aware that speed and comfort were important when he commented, 'The public will always prefer the conveyance which is most nearly perfect, and speed, within reasonable limits, is a material ingredient in the perfection of

travelling.' Brunel was as confident as ever, and suggested that a series of engine trials might help to satisfy the many sceptics who thought that the broad gauge was no more than an expensive folly. In retrospect, Brunel was by this time probably resigned to losing his broad-gauge argument: the offer of a trial was probably just a way of proving the superiority of his engines and it did nothing to address the problem of two incompatible gauges. The commissioners, in true British fashion, were unable to make a decision and agreed to the trial. It would be run between Paddington and Didcot and between York and Darlington hauling loads of 60, 70 and 80 tons. Using one of the very successful 'Fire Fly' engines, *Ixion*, the GWR trials were run between Paddington and Didcot on 16 and 17 December 1845, and, in typical Brunel spirit, the broad gauge won hands down. Nevertheless, the commission, while admitting that the broad gauge was supreme in speed and safety, came down in favour of the narrow gauge, stating that 'the gauge of 4ft 8½in be declared by the Legislature to be the gauge to be used on all public railways' then under construction in Great Britain.

The Board of Trade did not totally agree, and although it passed an act making it unlawful to construct any new railways in Britain at a gauge other then 4ft 8½in, it gave exception to lines in the West Country and South Wales. Against much opposition, acts were obtained by the Great Western in 1846 for broad-gauge lines in the Midlands, South Wales, Devon and Cornwall. However, the Great Western gained its first narrow-gauge tracks on 1 September 1854 when it absorbed the narrow-gauge Shrewsbury & Chester and Shrewsbury & Birmingham Railways. In 1855 the first narrow-gauge engines were built at Swindon.

The commission had also insisted that the Oxford, Worcester & Wolverhampton Railway and the Oxford & Rugby Railway should be laid with mixed-gauge track. Although the mixed gauge was installed and used on the Oxford & Rugby, very little of the OW&W route was mixed. Some broad-gauge rail was installed, but it was worked from its opening as a narrow-gauge line. The first section of mixed-gauge track had been laid between Cheltenham and Gloucester in 1847 to allow Great Western broad-gauge trains to traverse the existing Birmingham & Gloucester railway between these two points. Narrow-gauge services were inaugurated on 1 October 1861, with three daily through services in each direction between Birkenhead, Wolverhampton and Paddington.

The problems caused by lack of through working and the subsequent loss of revenue probably caused the Great Western board many sleepless nights. At this time there were at least 26 breaks of gauge, and by about 1865 the board probably realised that it was bound to lose and that the end of the broad gauge was inevitable. In 1865 the Great Western was operating a total of 1,250 miles of track, comprising 598 miles of broad, 236 miles of mixed, and 416 miles of narrow gauge. At last the Great Western board 'bit the bullet', and in April 1869 the Oxford, Birmingham and Wolverhampton route was converted to narrow gauge, thus allowing, for the first time, through services between Paddington and Birkenhead. During the weekend of 11-13 May 1872, the whole of the South Wales main line, together with all of the connecting branches, comprising 188 miles of double and 48 miles of single track was converted from broad to narrow gauge.

Broad-gauge working north of Didcot Junction came to an end on 26 November 1872, when the broad-gauge rails were removed between Didcot and Oxford. On the same date, the old broad-gauge terminus at Oxford was closed: it had never been converted and had been used as a goods depot since the opening of the line to Birmingham on 1 October 1852. Progress continued, and in 1874 the broad gauge was removed in Somerset, Wiltshire and

Dorset — between Westbury and Weymouth, and Chippenham and Salisbury. It must have been with some sadness that Gooch saw his broad gauge being truncated, as he noted in his diary:

'During June this year we narrowed a large part of the broad gauge, all south of our main line between London and Bristol: it was done very well by the staff. Thus is that poor broad gauge gradually dying out. It now only exists on our main line between London and Bristol, and the Windsor and Henly [sic] branches, and as we are mixing the whole of the bd [sic] gauge left by the end of this year we will have narrow gauge over the whole of our system.'

By April 1875 the broad-gauge route mileage had been reduced to single figures, but this was short lived, as on 1 January 1876 the Bristol & Exeter Railway was amalgamated with the GWR. One month later the South Devon Railway was also amalgamated, and with the GWR taking over working of the Cornwall Railway, the broad-gauge mileage increased to 327. However, conversion had taken its toll, and even with this increased figure the broad gauge was still in the minority. In 1876 the mixed-gauge mileage, which included the jointly-owned West Cornwall Railway, stood at 219, while the narrow-gauge lines totalled 1,421 miles.

The spread of the narrow gauge had been rapid, and by the summer of 1877, of the 51 passenger trains leaving Paddington daily, only 12 were still broad-gauge. The last broad-gauge line to be constructed by the Great Western was the St Ives branch, which opened for traffic on 1 June 1877. By 1887 there were just six broad-gauge express passenger services in each direction between London and Bristol, of which four ran right through to Penzance. During the same year, a new service to and from Plymouth, known as the

'Jubilee', was added to the timetable, and in 1890 a new service to Penzance, the 'Cornishman', was introduced.

The 'Flying Dutchman', the 11.45am train to Plymouth and Penzance, had a booked time of 87min between Paddington and Swindon. All other passenger services at this time were narrow-gauge. The 'Flying Dutchman' is synonymous with the broad gauge. It was introduced by the GWR in 1861 and initially ran to Torquay, with a timing of 4hr 30min in each direction, with a slow connection continuing to Plymouth. In 1865 the 'Dutchman' ran as an express through to Plymouth (Millbay), taking just 6hr 25min. It was withdrawn during 1868, but in June 1869 it was reinstated and by 1871 was timed to run between Paddington and Plymouth in just 6hr 15min. The 'Zulu' was introduced in 1880 and ran to the same schedule as the 'Flying Dutchman'; however, the Up service started from Penzance, departing at 11.15am. These two services were the last of the first and second-class-only trains, both eventually succumbing to carry third-class passengers, the 'Zulu' in 1889 and the 'Dutchman' in 1890.

The decline of the broad gauge continued, and by 1891 just 171 miles were left, comprising just 42 miles of double and 129 miles of single track. All the remaining broad-gauge mileage was located west of Exeter, with the exception of the 12½-mile section from Taunton to Chard, which had been retained by the Great Western to counter the threat of the London & South Western in obtaining running powers over the branch (it was eventually converted over the weekend of 18-20 July 1891). At their meeting of 19 March 1891, the Great Western Board agreed that the final conversion should take place in May 1892, forming a Gauge sub-committee to oversee the conversion.

Left: A photo of 'Star' class 2-2-2 *Load Star*, off the rails near Carmarthen on 3 January 1855. After working into Carmarthen with the 9.15am service from Haverfordwest, the engine was found to have a broken right-hand leading spring. Instead of changing engines, a temporary repair was undertaken at Carmarthen using a block of wood to support the spring. *Load Star* was then dispatched back to Haverfordwest where even after several derailments it was pronounced OK, and proceeded to haul the 1.20pm Up service back to Carmarthen. About six miles out, it was once again derailed, this time taking its train with it. Luckily only the driver was hurt. Obviously a calculated risk that went wrong.
GWT Collection

CHAPTER 2

Great Western Broad Gauge Engines

Brunel was undoubtedly an excellent engineer, but when it came to choosing locomotives for the new railway, his judgement left a lot to be desired. He certainly liked to experiment, and unfortunately gave the manufacturers an almost impossible task in his specifications for the first locomotives. He did not design or produce drawings for any locomotives, leaving these to the various manufacturers.

He did however set these parameters: 'A velocity of 30 miles per hour to be considered as the standard velocity, and this to be attained without requiring the piston to travel at a greater rate than 280ft per minute. The engine to be of such dimension and power as to exert and maintain without difficulty — with the pressure of steam in the boiler not exceeding 50lb upon the square inch, and with a velocity of 30 miles per hour — a force

Below: The engine *Vulcan* was built by Charles Tayleur & Co of Newton-le-Willows as a 2-2-2 well tank with 8ft driving wheels, and was delivered to the Great Western at West Drayton on 25 November 1837. *Vulcan*, which cost £1,569 11s plus £400 for the tender, was the first engine to be tried in steam when on 28 December 1837 it ran for a short distance near Iver, Bucks. The photo is dated 1858 and shows the engine in later condition, having been withdrawn from stock in 1843 and reinstated in 1846 after conversion to a back tank. *Vulcan* was withdrawn from service in April 1868, having amassed 171,801 miles in service, but saw further use as a stationary boiler at Reading until July 1870.
GWT Collection

Above right: Apart from the 'Stars', the most successful of the early engines were the 62 members of the 'Fire Fly' class. These 2-2-2s were designed by Gooch and built by no less than seven different manufacturers between March 1840 and December 1842. The first member of the class, *Fire Fly*, was built by Jones, Turner & Evans and delivered on 12 March 1840. It cost the Great Western £1,735 and is pictured here minus the tender which cost £420. On 17 March 1840, hauling a directors' train from Reading to Paddington, the engine reportedly reached a maximum speed of 58mph east of Twyford. The class was used all over the system on many of the main-line passenger services until being replaced by the more powerful 'Iron Duke' class. *Fire Fly* was withdrawn in July 1870 and cut up in November of the same year, having run 378,801 miles in service. A replica *Fire Fly* is under construction at Didcot Railway Centre. *Ian Allan/Bucknall Collection*

Right: Boiler explosions were not uncommon in the early days of the Great Western. Pictured here is *Leopard* looking in rather a sorry state after its boiler exploded at Bristol in 1857. The engine, a member of the 'Fire Fly' class, was built by Sharp, Roberts & Co and was delivered in May 1840. It was subsequently rebuilt with a steel firebox and was withdrawn from service in December 1878, then sold on to Candy & Co in January 1879. *GWT Collection*

of traction equal to 800lb upon a level independent of the power required to move its own weight and that of the tender with a supply of fuel and water for one hour's consumption. The weight of the engine, exclusive of the tender, but in other respects supplied with water and fuel for work, not to exceed 10½ tons, and if above 8 tons to be carried on six wheels.'

The result was a series of locomotives with large wheels and small boilers, hardly a winning combination. In his defence, Brunel had to have some form of motive power in order to run the services, and any locomotive design was at this time in its infancy.

On 25 August 1836, the company submitted this report to its shareholders: 'Difficulties and objections were at first supposed by some persons to exist in the construction of engines for the increased width of rails, but the directors have pleasure in stating that several of the most experienced locomotive engine manufacturers in the north have undertaken to construct these, and several are now contracted for, adapted to the peculiar track and dimensions of this railway, calculated for a minimum velocity of thirty miles an hour.'

It is doubtful whether some of these early designs even reached the minimum velocity of 30mph. The appointment of 21-year-old Daniel Gooch as locomotive superintendent on 18 August 1837, at a salary of £300 per annum, brought a degree of stability to the locomotive department, but it was to be several years before he really made his mark. His early impressions of the first locomotives were not good; as his diary states: 'I was not much pleased with the design of the engines ordered. They had

Above: North Star was delivered by barge to Maidenhead from the makers Robert Stephenson & Co on 28 November 1837. This was the first engine on the company's books. It was originally ordered for the 5ft 6in gauge New Orleans Railway, but the order was cancelled and the engine was sold to the Great Western. Its 6ft 6in driving wheels were altered to 7ft 0in and the gauge widened to run on Brunel's broad gauge. *North Star*, together with its 11 sister engines, was very successful and at times kept the Great Western going. It was withdrawn in December 1870 with a final mileage of 428,848. In 1849 several of the class were fitted with longer boilers and frames and the photo shows the engine in this later condition. *GWT Collection*

very small boilers and cylinders and very large wheels…I felt very uneasy about the working of these machines, feeling sure that they would have enough to do to drive themselves along the road.'

His misgivings were soon to prove alarmingly true. For the opening of the railway, the Great Western had ordered nine 2-2-2 locomotives from no less than four different companies. Lot 1 comprised one engine from Stephenson's, three from Tayleur, two from Mather, Dixon & Co, and three from Sharp, Roberts. The first two engines, *Vulcan* and *Premier*, according to official records, arrived at West Drayton on 25 November 1837, but

Bottom left: 'Fire Fly' class *Centaur* was built by Nasmyth, Gaskell & Co and delivered in December 1841. The 'Fire Fly' class was Gooch's first effort at standardisation. The class was fitted with 7ft driving wheels, which unlike many of the early engines, were flanged. In this photograph the engine is coupled to a four-wheeled tender which is fitted with a porter's 'iron coffin' seat. *Centaur* ceased work in November 1867 and was then used as a stationary boiler at Swindon. Interestingly, it was not officially withdrawn from stock until July 1870. *Ian Allan/Bucknall Collection*

Left: Towards the end of their life, a number of the 'Fire Fly' class engines were rebuilt at Swindon. Seen here after rebuilding is *Tiger*, built by Sharp, Roberts & Co in April 1840 and rebuilt in November 1864 with a round-topped firebox and lengthened sandwich frames, with the addition of a cab for the crew. It is interesting to note that many of these early engines were withdrawn from service and stored. *Tiger* is a typical example: it ceased work in December 1873 after completing 255,735 miles in service, and was sold to Fielding & Platt in July 1875. *GWT Collection*

it has been suggested that they actually arrived on 10 November after the six-day sea journey from Liverpool to London. *Vulcan* was built by Charles Tayleur & Co at the Vulcan Foundry, Newton-le-Willows, and *Premier* by Mather, Dixon & Co of Liverpool. Both engines were delivered to the Thames (the voyage from Liverpool was via the north coast of Scotland) and transferred to a canal barge for their trip up the Grand Union Canal to West Drayton. The contract price for *Vulcan* was £1,569 11s 0d, plus £400 for the tender.

Three days later, on 28 November, the famous *North Star* arrived at Maidenhead. It was despatched by sea from Robert Stephenson's factory at Newcastle to the Thames, whence it too was barged up the river to Maidenhead. Although it was the third engine to arrive, *North Star* was actually the first on the books of the company. She was first steamed by the Great Western on 15 January 1838. *North Star* had actually been constructed for the 5ft 6in New Orleans Railway, but when that order was cancelled due to financial problems, it was sold to the Great Western and converted to 7ft gauge. An article in the 1895 *Great Western Railway Magazine* suggests that the engine was actually shipped to the United States, but not being delivered to the company, was returned to Stephenson's. On 16 January the company celebrated the locomotive's steaming with a dinner at West Drayton (the then locomotive headquarters). Gooch noted in his diary: 'Some Irish gentlemen took more wine than was good for them, and amused themselves by dancing an Irish war dance on our hats, which happened to be piled up in a corner of the room. I was rather disgusted with the termination of our dinner, and resolved never to have anything to do with another. I was one of the stewards.'

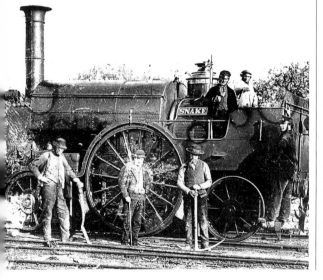

Left: Snake was built by the Haigh Foundry and delivered to the Great Western on 7 September 1838. Originally fitted with 6ft 6in wheels geared up in ratio of 3:2, in 1839 *Snake* and its sister engine *Viper* were rebuilt, the gearing was removed and possibly at this time they were fitted with 6ft driving wheels. In 1846 both engines were put to work on the South Devon Railway, apparently being renamed *Exe* and *Teign* respectively. Records indicate that *Teign* hauled the first passenger service from Exeter to Teignmouth on 30 May 1846. Within a few years, both engines had returned to work in the Thames Valley, the original names were reinstated, and on 27 July 1850 both were reported in steam at Slough. This picture shows *Snake* in what was probably its final condition, shunting in the old broad-gauge station at Oxford (Grandpont) in around 1865. *Snake* ceased work in December 1869 with a final mileage of 408,248 and *Viper* with 293,011 miles in January 1868. *Viper* was used for a time as a stationary boiler at Shrewsbury. *GWT Collection*

The end of November was a busy time for the newly established locomotive department, for on the 30th, two more Vulcan engines, *Bacchus* and *Aeolus*, were delivered. These early locomotives were delivered in parts and assembled on site. There was actually no track at West Drayton at this time, and it was not until May 1838 that tracklaying had progressed enough for any of the newly arrived locomotives to be run for any distance. Progress reports show that on 1 April 1838 only eight miles of track had been laid between Paddington and West Drayton.

According to Great Western records, the first trial runs of *Vulcan* and *Premier* were made over about 1¼ miles of line at West Drayton on 9 January 1838. The track adjacent to the shed must have been poor, as apparently both locomotives were derailed as they left the shed, but once out, Gooch reports that 'they performed beautifully, and we had a very interesting drive'.

West Drayton was the company's locomotive headquarters, with a small shed and coke ovens, until the new engine house at Paddington was opened in May 1838. As the line was extended westwards, temporary engine servicing points were also set up at Maidenhead, Twyford, Steventon, Faringdon Road and Hay Lane. These did not last long, and permanent engine sheds were established at Paddington in 1838 (replaced by Westbourne Park in 1855), and during 1840 at Slough, Reading, Bath and Bristol.

The first trial run of *North Star* is mentioned by Gibbs (a director of the GWR) as being on 1 May: 'Went today to Maidenhead and found two engines out for the first time with steam up. Brunel and his wife and Saunders were there, and the trial went off exceedingly well. I rode on the *North Star*, and found it very trying as I was not well, but the motion was very agreeable.' (Charles Saunders was the company secretary.)

Apart from *Vulcan*, five other Tayleur's engines were purchased: *Aeolus, Bacchus, Apollo, Neptune* and *Venus*. The Tayleur engines were generally poor. In a report dated 2 January 1839, Gooch states that of the six, '*Venus* is the worst engine delivered by Tayleur; I have been unable to make any use of her as a regular train engine, but we have kept her as a pilot at Maidenhead.' Mather, Dixon & Co supplied six engines (*Premier, Ariel, Ajax, Mars, Planet* and *Mercury*), and Sharp, Roberts supplied three (*Lion, Atlas* and *Eagle*).

The Haigh Foundry supplied a further two, *Viper* and *Snake*, which were delivered in August and September 1838 and like many of the others soon proved to be useless: 'Neither of these engines are sufficiently to be depended on to run the trains.' They were rebuilt in 1839/40, and in 1846 they were working on the South Devon Railway, having been renamed *Teign* and *Exe*. Around 1851 they reverted to their original names, and ended their days working in the Thames Valley and on the Oxford Railway.

R. & W. Hawthorn supplied the engines *Thunderer* in March 1838 and *Hurricane* in October 1838, but by far the best of the bunch were the six from Robert Stephenson & Co: *North Star, Morning Star, Evening Star, Dog Star, Polar Star* and *Red Star*. Costing around £2,500 each, they were the most expensive, but probably the most reliable. As the saying goes, 'you get what you pay for'. *North Star* was eventually withdrawn from service in December 1870, having amassed some 429,000 miles in service. *Ariel* and *Premier*, which ran only 7,840 and 14,789 miles respectively, together with *Ajax, Mars,*

Planet and *Neptune* were all reported to have been taken out of use during 1840 — not a very good start!

By the end of May 1838, the Great Western Railway was ready for operation, albeit just the 22½ mile section from Paddington to a temporary station at Maidenhead. Of the initial locomotive order, only 10 had been delivered for the opening: *Vulcan, Aeolus, Bacchus, Apollo, Neptune, Premier, Ariel, Lion, Thunderer* and *North Star.*

On 31 May, an experimental train of six coaches carrying directors and MPs and hauled by the engine *North Star* left Paddington at 11am. With Brunel on the footplate, the 22½ mile journey was completed in 47min. Francis Whishaw, inventor of the hydraulic telegraph and author of the book *Railways of Great Britain and Ireland* (published 1840), also recorded three experimental runs between Paddington and Maidenhead on 4 June, 21 July and 6 November behind the engine *Aeolus.* He noted that on 6 November, with a load of 44,440lb (about 20 tons), a top speed of 48mph was attained on the approach to Drayton, and that for the round trip of about 45 miles the engine consumed 15.70lb of coke per mile.

Passenger services opened on 4 June 1838. The first train comprised seven vehicles, and was hauled by the engine *Aeolus.* It left Paddington at 8am with about 200 passengers on board. Unfortunately, at West Drayton, a leaky tube extinguished the fire and the train had to be unceremoniously pushed to Maidenhead by the next one, causing a delay of about 76min. This was not a very auspicious start, but a prelude to the problems yet to come. The first Up service left Maidenhead at 8am pulled by the engine *Apollo* and with two first-class, two second-class and two open carriages. Altogether on the first day the railway carried 1,479 passengers, with receipts totalling £226. There were initially just eight services in each direction daily, and, though these were advertised in local newspapers and the London *Times*, no official timetables were published until 1 May 1839. This was entirely due to the

Above: One of the fourth lot of 'Standard Goods' 0-6-0s, *Pearl* is pictured here at Weymouth in the 1860s. Built at Swindon in May 1852, *Pearl* was one of 102 'Standard Goods' engines with 5ft 0in driving wheels built at Swindon in seven lots between May 1852 and March 1863. They became part of the 'Caesar' class and saw use on goods services over the whole of the broad-gauge system. *Pearl* in this picture is fitted with a spectacle plate with a simple curved top and later-type chimney. Many of these early engines were apparently cut up long before they were officially withdrawn from service: *Pearl* was cut up in February 1878 but not taken off the books until June 1878. Final mileage in service is recorded as 395,773. *GWT Collection*

Below: Europa, built in March 1853 as part of the fifth lot of 'Standard Goods' engines, was rebuilt in July 1869 and fitted with an Armstrong designed cab and a new boiler. The photograph shows the engine in its rebuilt state at Swindon and after withdrawal from service. The Swindon builder's plate on the running plate is dated July 1869. *Europa* was the only one of the 102 engines to be rebuilt. It survived to the end of the broad gauge and was reported as being the last broad-gauge engine to leave Plymouth, working Up to Swindon on the morning of 21 May 1892. Mileage from July 1869 is recorded as 478,251. *GWT Collection*

Left: Hecuba, pictured here at Newton Abbot, was built in November 1853. The engine has its original open cab with no spectacle plate, and its original pattern chimney. It is possibly one of the earliest photographs in the book, dating from around the late 1850s. The double diamond on the front buffer beam indicates that the engine is on branch-line working. *Hecuba* ceased work in June 1873, having run 408,788 miles in service, and was sold on 8 August 1873 to the Dinas Main Coal Co for use as a colliery winding engine at a cost of £850. *Ian Allan/Bucknall Collection*

Centre left: The sixth lot 'Standard Goods' comprised 40 engines built between February 1854 and June 1857. *Nemesis*, pictured here at Warminster on the Salisbury branch, was built in January 1855, and withdrawn after completing 421,382 miles in service in November 1877. *The late Rev J. Ashford/A. Kingdom Collection*

Below: The first of the seventh lot engines to be turned out was *Liffey*, seen here in fully-lined livery and with an open cab and elegant reverse curves to the spectacle plate. Built at Swindon in August 1857, it ceased work in March 1872. *Ian Allan/Bucknall Collection*

Above right: Seventh-lot 'Standard Goods' 0-6-0 *Tay*, built at Swindon in August 1858 and pictured here at Westbourne Park shed yard. The engine is in fully-lined livery; the two brass plates on the running board read 'Great Western Railway Co' and 'August 1858'. Here it is coupled to an ex-B&E tender. *Tay* ceased work in March 1881, but was not officially withdrawn from service until June. Final mileage is recorded as 440,688. Note the small sandbox outside the cab, a feature not fitted to all of the class. *GWT Collection*

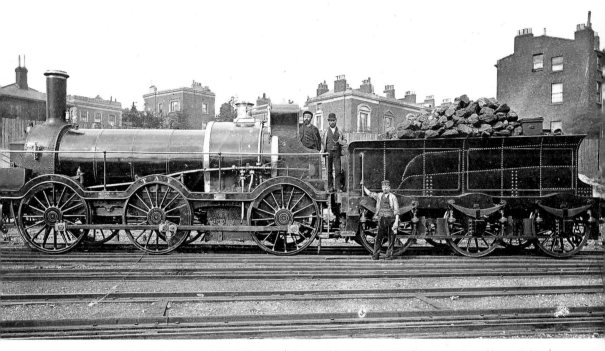

Below: Xerxes was one of the 10th-lot 'Standard Goods' built at Swindon in January 1863. It is seen here in the yard at Westbourne Park. These later engines had welded plate frames. It is also fitted with a later-type cab, and is coupled to an ex-B&E tender. *Xerxes* was withdrawn from service in December 1882. *Ian Allan Library*

1848, it was finally withdrawn in December 1873. *Caliban* was withdrawn in April 1873 and sold to the Severn Tunnel Railway, but was apparently returned to GWR stock in September 1873 before it was withdrawn once again. The next batch of goods engines, the 'Caesar' class 0-6-0s, were not constructed until 1851. As with the previous goods classes, Gooch was gradually improving his designs, the eight members of the class being a further development of the 'Pyracmon' class. *Dido* was the first of the class, constructed in June 1851, but the longest serving was *Caesar*. Built in August 1851, it was not withdrawn until June 1880. The average mileage for the class was about 400,000.

Below: The 10 engines of the 'Waverley' class were built in 1855 by Robert Stephenson & Co of Newcastle. These large 4-4-0s had 7ft 0in coupled wheels and were based mainly at Swindon for working services to South Wales, Gloucester and Bristol. This photograph shows the engine *Rob Roy* coupled to a contemporary tender. The white diamonds indicate that the engine is on branch-line working. Note also the complete lack of protection for the crew. Built in April 1855, *Rob Roy* was withdrawn in February 1872. *GWT Collection*

Bottom: The 'Waverley' class were the only 4-4-0 tender engines to run on the broad gauge. *Antiquary* was the last built, in June 1855, and was withdrawn in June 1876. It is pictured here in original condition with an early pattern chimney and no spectacle plates. Notice also its full-length brass running board. Its final mileage is recorded as 526,458. *GWT Collection*

Above: This rather faded picture shows the engine *Ivanhoe*. Built at Newcastle in March 1855, it was withdrawn from service in September 1876, having completed 523,862 miles.
Ian Allan/Bucknall Collection

Right: Crowds pose for the photographer at the scene of an accident at Bullo Pill on 5 November 1868. *Rob Roy*, a 'Waverley' class 4-4-0 hauling the 5pm Up service from Milford, comprising three coaches and a luggage van, ran at speed into the rear of a special goods and cattle train hauled by *Tantalus* at Bullo Pill Junction, some 12 miles south of Gloucester. The cattle train had stalled in the section. Several men travelling in the rear van of the cattle train died, many of the cattle wagons were extensively damaged, and about 36 cattle killed. The accident took place at about 10pm, and the driver of *Rob Roy* reported a very weak rear light on the goods train which resulted in him not seeing it until it was too late. *Rob Roy* was repaired and was eventually withdrawn in February 1872.
GW Trust Collection

At a total of 102 locomotives, by far the most numerous broad-gauge class built by the Great Western was the 0-6-0 known as Gooch's 'Standard Goods'. This class, built at Swindon, comprised seven lots and was constructed between May 1852 and March 1863. As with the previous goods engines, these were fitted with inside frames. They were particularly successful, working over much of the system. Great Western records indicate that the engine *Europa*, built in March 1853, was the last in the class to be withdrawn. It was the very last broad-gauge engine to work from Plymouth when it departed for Swindon at about 4am on 21 May 1892. It was also the only member of the class to be rebuilt, the work being undertaken in June 1869.

During 1860, the Great Western decided to substitute coal for coke, which had been used as a fuel from the railway's opening in 1838. At first coke ovens were established at West Drayton, but around 1842 new ovens were constructed at Bristol and the West Drayton ovens were closed. The coal for coking was obtained from the Rhondda Valley and shipped to Bristol by boat across the Severn estuary from Cardiff. Brunel had apparently tried to use anthracite coal in some of the early engines, but soon found that it tended to crumble into powder and was carried through the tubes, eventually blocking up the smokebox after just a few miles. It was to take nearly 20 years of experimentation to solve the problem of burning bituminous coal in locomotive fireboxes.

The last engines to be designed by Gooch were the 22 members of the 'Metropolitan' class. These 2-4-0 tanks were constructed between 1862 and 1864, and were the only broad-gauge engines built for the Great Western to have outside cylinders. Seven were constructed by the Vulcan Foundry between June and August 1862, six by Kitson & Co of Leeds between June and September 1862, and 10 at Swindon between July 1863 and October 1864.

The engines were constructed to work over the widened lines of the Metropolitan Railway and were the first to be built with condensing apparatus. The broad gauge was removed from the Metropolitan in 15 March 1869, after which date many of the class had their condensing apparatus removed and seven of the class were converted to tender engines. Put to use on other work, all 22 had been withdrawn by 1877.

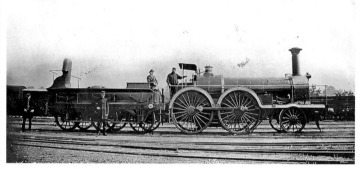

Left: The 2-4-0 'Victoria' class comprised 18 engines with 6ft 6in coupled wheels which were built at Swindon in two lots, eight in 1856 under lot five, and 10 in 1863/4 under lot six. Pictured here is the engine *Napoleon*, one of the first batch, which was built at Swindon in August 1856. It is shown here in slightly later condition, fitted with an extended spectacle plate forming a very basic cab. *Napoleon* ceased work in December 1880 with a final mileage of 548,037. *Ian Allan Library*

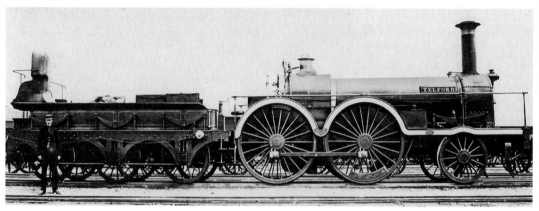

Above: Telford was one of the second batch of the 'Victoria' class. Built in April 1864, it is seen here as built, without cab and coupled to an express-type tender with travelling porter's seat and bell. Used on intermediate services, a number of the class were used on the Weymouth line. *Telford* ceased work in February 1879 with a mileage of 360,165, but according to the records was not officially withdrawn until December of that year. *GWT Collection*

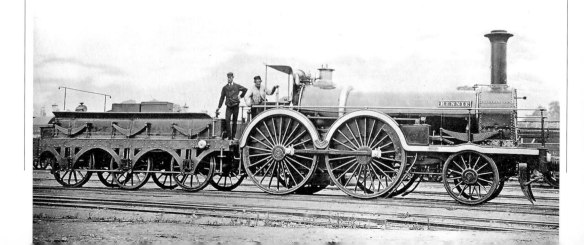

Top: An unidentified Gooch 'Rover' class 2-2-2 speeds past Ealing Broadway with a down service in 1891/2. The train comprises both narrow bodied convertible and broad gauge stock. The up and down narrow gauge relief lines were opened between Portobello and Southall on 1 October 1877. *GWT Collection*

Above: Though the original *Great Western* was withdrawn in 1870, a new *Great Western* was one of 24 engines built from 1871 and known as the 'Iron Duke renewals' or 'Rover' class. The second *Great Western* was turned out from Swindon in May 1888 and was the penultimate purely broad-gauge engine to be constructed. Understandably, its final recorded mileage was just 202,342. It is seen standing outside the works at Swindon and is fitted with a larger boiler and the final type of chimney. Unlike their earlier counterparts which had brakes on only one side of the tender, all of the 'Rovers' were fitted with vacuum brakes on the driving and trailing axles and all the tender wheels. *GWT Collection*

Left: The last of the 'Rover' Iron Duke renewals to be constructed was *Tornado*, built at Swindon in July 1888 and pictured here at Exeter in around 1890. The engine is fitted with a large capacity boiler and a 3,000gal tender. *Tornado* spent most of its short life allocated to Bristol. It was withdrawn after just 3 years 10 months in service, having amassed a running total of 192,203 miles. *Ian Allan Library*

Below left: The Down 'Flying Dutchman', hauled by *Inkermann*, speeds past the signal cabin at Worle Junction. The driver, G. Eggar, can be seen waving to the photographer. *Rev A. H. Malan/ GWT Collection*

Right: The Up 'North Mail' hauled by *Warlock* is seen here near Exminster on 5 May 1891. Warlock was built in November 1876 and was rebuilt with a larger boiler in September 1888. Its mileage after March 1888 was recorded as 179,265. The first vehicle on the train appears to be a Travelling Post Office. Notice the broad-gauge track which at this point has been laid using chairs and sleepers. *Ian Allan/Bucknall Collection*

Above: A splendid view of the Down 'Cornishman' hauled by the engine *Emperor* at Uphill Junction, probably in around May 1892. On the left is a narrow-gauge goods waiting to come off the Weston Branch. It appears to be hauled by an Armstrong 'Standard Goods' convertible 0-6-0. *Rev A. H. Malan/GWT Collection*

Broad-Gauge Convertibles

Apart from the purely broad-gauge engines built for and by the Great Western, 112 'Convertible' engines were constructed by the company from 1876 at Swindon. It was obvious by this time that the end of the broad gauge was in sight, so the company decided not to produce any new designs of broad-gauge locomotives but to adapt a number of narrow-gauge designs to run on the broad gauge.

The first 10 to be outshopped were Armstrong double-frame 0-6-0 saddle tanks, which were constructed between October and December 1876. They were fitted with broad-gauge axles and wheels outside the frames. During November and December 1878 a further five were similarly treated.

As some of the older broad-gauge engines were taken out of service, they were replaced by a further batch of convertible engines, comprising a further 35 Armstrong 0-6-0 saddle tanks and 20 Armstrong 0-6-0 double-framed Standard Goods. These 55 had run previously as narrow-gauge engines and were converted to run on broad-gauge tracks between 1884 and 1888. In June 1877 Joseph Armstrong died. He was replaced as Locomotive Superintendent by William Dean, who had been his assistant at Swindon.

Dean initially continued to construct Armstrong designs, but between 1885 and 1891, 41 convertibles designed by Dean were turned out from Swindon. Unlike the previous convertibles,

Above: In the last years of the broad gauge the Great Western needed a number of extra locomotives to replace some of the worn-out older classes. In 1884, 20 of the Armstrong 'Standard Goods' 0-6-0s, built at Swindon in 1876 as narrow-gauge engines, were converted to run on the broad gauge. Pictured here is No 1208, built at Swindon in August 1876 and converted for use on the broad gauge in May 1884. All 20 were fitted with cabs and put to use working goods services between Plymouth and London. With the end of the broad gauge in May 1892, the 20 engines were converted back to run on the narrow or standard gauge, No 1208 being completed on 30 June 1892. As a broad-gauge engine, it ran for 258,265 miles. It was finally withdrawn from service in December 1919 with a total mileage recorded as 1,038,425.
Ian Allan/Bucknall Collection

these were constructed as broad-gauge engines. The first 10 were 2-4-0 side tanks and were completed during April/May 1885. They had double frames and 5ft 1in coupled wheels. Five of the class were converted to tender engines, three during 1890 and two in 1891, for use on the 'Cornishman' between Exeter and Plymouth. All of the class were converted to tender engines after May 1892.

The final batch of 20 passenger tank engines was constructed at Swindon between September 1888 and July 1889. Again designed by Dean, the first 19 were 0-4-2 saddle tanks with 5ft 0in coupled wheels. This design apparently proved to be unstable, so the final engine was turned out as an 0-4-4 with side and back tanks, and between 1890 and 1891 all the other 19 were converted. Even after the alterations they were still unstable, and

Right: An unidentified Armstrong 'Standard Goods' convertible passes West Ealing in around 1890 with a short goods train. *Ian Allan/Bucknall Collection*

Centre right: In May 1886 the Great Western built two experimental four-cylinder tandem compounds, one for each gauge. Designed by Dean, No 8 was a 2-4-0 tender engine and fitted with 7ft 0½ in coupled wheels. The two low-pressure cylinders were placed in front, each having two piston rods which ran outside the high-pressure cylinders connecting with common cross heads. This arrangement gave continual trouble: during its trials the low-pressure pistons and cylinder covers shattered. The engine became something of a 'white elephant' — it never saw regular use, running for only 3,350 miles, and spent much of its time in store. It was partially dismantled in May 1892, and in May 1894 some of its parts were used to construct a 4-4-0 standard gauge 'renewal'. *GWT Collection*

Below: No 14 was built at Swindon in May 1888, one of two 2-4-0 tender engines with 7ft 0½in coupled wheels built by Dean to work the heavy 3pm Up express service from Bristol to Swindon. The photograph shows the engine as new at Swindon. It was intended to convert this engine and its sister engine No 16 to standard gauge; neither was actually converted, but in 1894 parts from both were used to construct two new standard-gauge 4-4-0 renewals. *GWT Collection*

Left: No 14 at speed on an Up express service near Bathampton — possibly the 3pm service from Bristol to Paddington. No 14 was withdrawn from service on 21 May 1892 with a final mileage recorded as 58,796.
Ian Allan/Bucknall Collection

Below: No 16 was the sister engine to No 14, and was built at Swindon in June 1888. It is seen here at Bristol in around 1890. The two engines were unusually fitted with plate inner frames and slotted sandwich outer, the wheels being outside the frames. No 16 was withdrawn on 21 May 1892 with a mileage of 86,978. *GWT Collection*

Left: No 1236 was an Armstrong Standard 'Buffalo' class 0-6-0ST with 4ft 6in coupled wheels. Built at Swindon in December 1876 at a cost of £1,470, it was one of 10 members of the class to be constructed with broad-gauge axles. It was converted to standard gauge in June 1892. *Ian Allan/Bucknall Collection*

between 1899 and 1902 were again altered into 4-4-0 tender engines.

The remaining 11 convertible engines were all designed by Dean and built at Swindon between May 1886 and August 1891 for use on express passenger services between London, Bristol and Newton Abbot.

No 8 was built in May 1886. This 2-4-0 tender engine was a four-cylinder compound with plate frames and 7ft 0½in driving wheels. Unfortunately, it proved to be a failure and never saw regular service. Ernest L. Ahrons in his articles 'Locomotive and Train Working in the Latter Part 19th Century' states that on a least two occasions the engine suffered severe piston failure, due to unequal expansion of the piston rods, which in turn caused excessive strain in the piston heads.

Nos 14 and 16 were constructed in May and June 1888. These two 2-4-0 tender engines were also fitted with 7ft 0½in diameter driving wheels and were built to haul the heavy 3pm Up express from Bristol to Paddington. They were stationed at Swindon for much of their working life, and were quite successful, but together with No 8, they were dismantled at Swindon Works in May 1892, and their parts reused to construct three new narrow-gauge engines.

The remaining eight convertibles, Nos 3021-8, were 2-2-2s with 7ft 8in driving wheels, and were constructed between April and August 1891. They were used to supplement the 'Rover' class engines on main-line services to the West until May 1892. All eight were converted to standard gauge, but as a class they were not particularly successful and proved to be very unstable. After No 3021 was derailed in Box Tunnel on 16 September 1893, it was decided to convert them all to 4-2-2 bogie singles.

Right: This picture shows No 1229, built at Swindon in the same lot (43) as No 1236, but in October 1876. Many of these convertibles worked in the West of England on both passenger and goods services. To operate the passenger services, a number had the rear coupling rods removed and ran, apparently much better, as 0-4-2s. No 1229 is seen here in steam and running as an 0-4-2ST. *Ian Allan/Bucknall Collection*

Below: During 1891 the Great Western temporarily fitted eight narrow-gauge 2-2-2s, Nos 3021-8, with broad-gauge wheels and axles, to supplement the service during the last months of broad-gauge operation. Pictured here at Swindon is No 3023: turned out in July 1891, it had double frames and 7ft 8½in driving wheels. As a broad-gauge engine it ran 28,946 miles. On 13 August 1892 it was converted to standard gauge, and on 10 October 1894 was rebuilt as a 4-2-2 at a cost of £1,599 and named *Swallow. R. de Lacy-Spencer/Ian Allan Library*

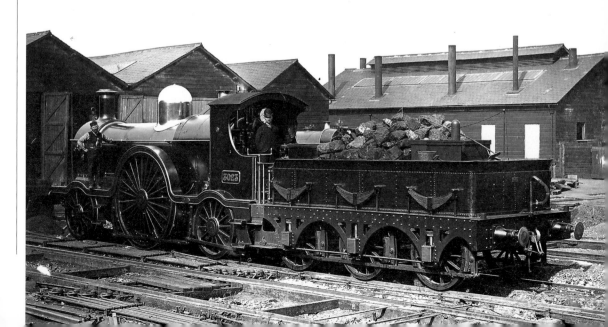

Top: A side view of No 3025, one of eight 2-2-2s temporarily converted to broad-gauge, shows the attractive lines of these engines. The plate on the running board gives the construction date, August 1891. Notice also the engine jack in its position on the running board — the Great Western Trust has a similar jack on show at Didcot. Converted back to standard gauge on 19 July 1892, this engine was rebuilt as a 4-2-2 on 24 November 1894. Broad-gauge mileage is recorded as 22,144. *Ian Allan Library*

Above: An unidentified member of the '3021' convertible class emerges from Sonning Cutting with a Down 'West of England' express during the last few months of the broad gauge. Typical of the period, its eight-coach train comprises narrow-bodied convertible coaches. Posing for the photographer are probably the PW inspector and his men — as can be seen, work is underway constructing the narrow gauge relief lines through the cutting. *Rob Tibbits*

Right: In 1885, the Great Western built 10 convertible 2-4-0 side tanks with 5ft 1in wheels for intermediate passenger work. In 1890/1, five of the class were rebuilt as tender engines for use on express services between Exeter and Plymouth. No 3510 was constructed in May 1885 and lasted to the end of the gauge as a 2-4-0 tank. In September 1892 it was converted to a 4-4-0 'Stella' class standard-gauge tender engine. *GWT Collection*

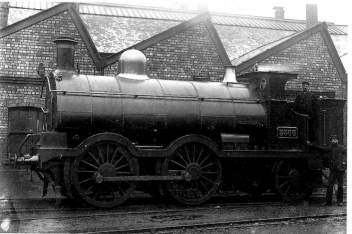

Centre right: No 3555 was one of the last batch of 20 passenger tank engines built for the broad gauge. Designed by Dean, these 0-4-2 saddle tanks were built to work services in South Devon and Cornwall. As saddle tanks they proved to be unstable, and the final locomotive, No 3560, was turned out as an 0-4-4 side and back tank; the other 19 were rebuilt in similar style during 1890/1. All were converted to standard gauge during 1892, but as a class they still suffered from poor riding, and between March 1899 and October 1900 all 20 were rebuilt as 4-4-0 tender engines. *Ian Allan Library*

Below: No 3560, built at Swindon in July 1889, was the only one of its class originally built as an 0-4-4 side and back tank. It is pictured around 1890. *Ian Allan Library*

CHAPTER 4

South Devon Railway Engines

With the completion of the Bristol & Exeter Railway, thoughts had turned to extending the line from Exeter through to Plymouth. The South Devon Railway, which was inaugurated on 4 July 1844, was opened to Teignmouth on 30 May 1846; to Newton (Abbot) on 30 December; to Totnes on 20 July 1847; to Laira Green, some two miles east of Plymouth, on 5 May 1848; and to Plymouth on 2 April 1849. The railway is particularly interesting as it was constructed to work on the Samuda Brothers' atmospheric principle. The system, which was patented in 1839, used the pressure of the atmosphere as a driving force, and required no locomotives as such. It had been installed on a short stretch of coastal railway in Ireland.

A large-diameter continuous cast-iron pipe (15in diameter on the South Devon) was laid between the rails. Inside the pipe was a close-fitting piston. At the top of the pipe was a continuous slit about 2½in wide, which allowed the piston to be connected via a sealing valve to a small four-wheeled carriage. The seal or flap which ran along the whole length of the pipe was made of leather.

Situated at intervals along the route were a series of atmospheric engine pumping houses. In these, stationary steam engines operated large pumps which were used to evacuate the air from in front of the piston, thereby creating a partial vacuum; the atmospheric pressure of the air behind the piston then drove the whole thing forward. The system had been tested on the West London Railway in February 1840, and the subsequent report stated that 'The experiments at Wormwood Scrubs have proved the practicality of giving motion to considerable loads, at a maximum velocity of 40mph.'

The idea was adopted at the company board meeting on 28 August 1844: 'Your directors…have resolved that the atmospheric system…should be adopted upon the whole of the line of the South Devon Railway.' It was Brunel's idea to use this system because of the steep gradients and sharp curves on the line, which he thought could not be worked using locomotives.

The first services between Exeter and Teignmouth were actually locomotive-hauled because the

Right: Ostrich was built for the South Devon Railway by William Fairbairn & Sons of Manchester. A 4-4-0ST based on Gooch's *Corsair* design, it was one of the first 12 engines supplied under the first contract and was delivered in August 1852. In a report on 'the present state of engines' dated Tuesday 10 October 1854, it 'had a piece of steel out of the tire'. Numbered 2104 by the Great Western, it was withdrawn in December 1877. *The late J. B. N. Ashford/by courtesy of A. Kingdom*

Left: A South Devon Railway train stands at Lifton on the Launceston branch, hauled by one of the early South Devon 4-4-0 saddle tanks, possibly *Ostrich*, built for the company by William Fairbairn & Sons in August 1852. The diamonds on the removable board on the buffer beam denote a branch-line train. The line from Launceston to Tavistock was opened on 1 July 1865 and converted during 20-23 May 1892. *GWT Collection*

Centre left: Aurora was one of the first batch of five engines supplied by Longridge & Co to the South Devon in January 1852. A 4-4-0ST with 5ft 9in coupled wheels, it was withdrawn as No 2099 in November 1878. These early SDR engines saw considerable use on branch-line services. On 10 October 1854, a report shows that *Aurora* was temporarily out of service: 'Broke clacks and pulled out fire at Kingsbridge Road this morning.' *The late J. B. N. Ashford/ by courtesy of A. Kingdom*

Below: The engine *Mazeppa* and crew pose for a photograph at Penryn about 1865. *Mazeppa* was built by Slaughter, Gruning & Co in May 1859 and withdrawn in June 1885. The first coach of the train is an early mail van. Note also the carriage destination board, lantern lights on the raised clerestory roof and fleur-de-lis on the upper panels. *Ian Allan/Bucknall Collection*

Above: Giraffe was built for the South Devon Railway by Slaughter, Gruning & Co in June 1859. Similar in design to the 1851 batch of engines, it was fitted with a full-length 1,100gal tank that extended from the back of the smokebox to the back of the firebox. The small seat behind the sandbox was used for manually pouring sand. The double diamonds on the buffer beam indicated that the engine is on branch-line duty.
GWT Collection

atmospheric system was not finished. The inaugural service over the 15-mile section between Exeter and Teignmouth, the 12.25pm to Teignmouth, departed from Exeter on 30 May 1846. It comprised nine carriages and was hauled by the Haigh Foundry 2-2-2 *Teign*. A sister engine named *Exe* was also used at this time. Both engines were on hire from the Great Western and had been renamed for the occasion.

The line was opened through to Newton on 30 December, the first service being hauled by the 'Sun' class 2-2-2 *Antelope*, one of five Great Western engines on hire to the company at this time. The first service from Exeter to Totnes on 20 July 1847 was also hauled by two Great Western engines, 'Leo' class 2-4-0 *Pisces* and 'Fire Fly' class 2-2-2 *Pegasus*.

Under the direction of the engineer James Pearson, a series of test trains using the atmospheric

principle was run during February 1847. The trials proved to be successful enough for atmospheric services to commence between Exeter and Teignmouth on Monday 13 September 1847. The system started well, but unfortunately for the company and also Brunel, it proved to be unreliable, and soon the company was losing money hand over fist. Had it worked, the system would have been cheap to run. However, general wear and tear of passing trains, and the problem of rats eating the leather, caused leakages of the seal. The problems became insurmountable and the whole exercise became an expensive failure, costing the company some £400,000. The atmospheric system lasted just eight months, and on 6 September 1848 the board decided that atmospheric traction would be abandoned. On Sunday 10 September 1848 services were operated using a number of loaned GWR engines.

The engines supplied by the Great Western were really unsuitable for the steep gradients on the line. To help alleviate the problem, Gooch designed two 4-4-0 saddle tanks, *Corsair* and *Brigand*, for the South Devon services. These were built at Swindon, and, unusually for the time, were fitted with swivelling front bogies. They were, to all intents and purposes, prototypes for future South Devon designs. Both

commenced working from Plymouth in 1849: *Corsair* was delivered in August and was initially fitted with a sledge brake. This was situated between the driving wheels and worked simply by pressing on the rails. The brake was not a success — when applied hard it apparently lifted the engine off the rails. *Brigand*, which was delivered in September, was fitted with conventional brake blocks on the back of the trailing wheels. The Gooch registers show that in July 1850 these Great Western engines were on loan to the South Devon Railway: 'Leo' class 2-4-0s *Aquarius, Buffalo, Capricornus, Dromedary, Elephant, Libra, Pisces, Scorpio* and *Taurus*, and 'Fire Fly' class 2-2-2 *Fire Ball*.

The loan agreement with the Great Western did not last for long, and on 1 July 1851 the South Devon Railway entered its own agreement with Edgar Evans of Wigan and Charles Geach of Birmingham for the supply of locomotives for the railway. The first order was for 12 passenger locomotives and four goods engines. This 'Comet' class comprised 4-4-0 saddle tanks, again with swivelling front bogies, and was based on the design of *Corsair* with inside sandwich frames. The passenger locomotives were constructed by four different builders (five by Longridge & Co of Bedlington; four by the Haigh Foundry, Wigan; two by Stothert & Slaughter of Bristol; and one by William Fairbairn & Sons of Manchester). They were delivered between 1851 and 1853. The four goods engines were 0-6-0 saddle tanks and were built by the Vulcan Foundry in 1854/5. One of the class, *Tornado*, suffered a major boiler explosion on 13 April 1860 while shunting at Totnes. Unfortunately, the driver was killed and the fireman seriously injured.

The second order placed by the company comprised 16 'Hawk' 4-4-0 class passenger engines, which were similar in design to the 'Comets', and a further eight 0-6-0ST goods engines. These were all built by Slaughter, Gruning & Co of Bristol, and delivered between 1859 and 1865. All 40 engines were designed by Gooch and were leased to the railway on a 10-year contract,

Right: No 2135 *Magpie* was built by Sharp, Stewart & Co in 1861 as a 4-4-0 side tank and was initially hired out to the Carmarthen & Cardigan Railway. In 1872 *Magpie* was sold to the South Devon Railway and altered to a 4-4-0ST. Taken over by the Great Western in September 1872 and numbered 2135, it was withdrawn from service in June 1889. It is pictured towards the end of its working life outside the shed at St Ives. *GWT Collection*

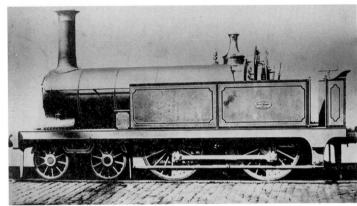

Right: Heron was built by Sharp, Stewart & Co in 1861 as a 4-4-0 side tank with 5ft 2in coupled wheels, and was used on the Carmarthen & Cardigan Railway until it was purchased by the South Devon Railway in September 1872. It is shown here in ex-works condition. *Ian Allan/Bucknall Collection*

with payment being based on the annual mileage run. Servicing was centred at Newton (Abbot), where the main South Devon workshops and locomotive running shed were established, probably soon after the atmospheric system was abandoned. A small two-road shed was opened at Exeter in May 1846, and for the banking engines at Totnes in July 1847. A much larger servicing facility, which eventually comprised two separate running sheds, was opened at Plymouth Millbay in June 1849.

On 6 May 1859, the engine *Elk*, a 4-4-0T built by Slaughter, Gruning in April 1859, was derailed as it approached Grove viaduct near St Germans. The engine and the first two coaches rolled down the 30ft embankment into the creek and sank in the adjacent mud. The driver, fireman and guard were killed. Another Slaughter, Gruning engine, *Hebe*, an 0-6-0ST, suffered a major boiler explosion while standing at Brent station on 22 November 1873. No one was hurt, and both engines survived to pass into Great Western ownership. Of the early engines, *Lance*, built by Longridge & Co in October 1851, was destroyed in a collision with two other locomotives, *Romulus* and *Brutus*, near St Germans on 2 December 1873.

On 1 July 1859, the contract with the leasing company was renewed for a further seven years, but when the contract came up for renewal on 1 July 1866, the South Devon Railway decided to take over the working itself and purchased the locomotives from the leasing company. On 1 January 1866, the narrow-gauge West Cornwall Railway was taken over by a Great Western, South Devon and Bristol & Exeter consortium. It was managed by the West Cornwall Committee which comprised members of all three companies, and locomotives were supplied by the South Devon. Broad-gauge rails were laid between Truro and Penzance in November 1866, but broad-gauge passenger services did not commence until 1 March 1867. At this time, South Devon locomotive livery comprised green boilers and brown frames. Later, engines were apparently turned out in dark green with black lining. The main running sheds in Cornwall were established at Truro by the Cornwall Railway. A two road shed was opened on 4 May 1859, and a small single-road shed at Liskeard opened on the same date. The Cornwall Railway also opened a two-road shed at Falmouth on 24 August 1863. A mixed-gauge shed was opened at Penzance by the Great Western in 1876.

Top: The South Devon Railway soon converted *Heron* to a 4-4-0 saddle tank with 5ft 3in coupled wheels. It is seen here in its final form with a large enclosed cab. *Heron* became GWR No 2134 in 1876, and was withdrawn from service in May 1892. *GWT Collection*

Above: The 0-6-0ST 4ft 6in goods engine *Una* was built by Slaughter, Gruning & Co for the Llynvi Valley Railway in 1862. It was one of three engines built for this railway, the others being *Rosa* and *Ada*. When the company combined with the Ogmore Valley to form the Llynvi & Ogmore Railway on 1 July 1866, it adopted the narrow gauge, and in April 1868 all three engines were swapped for four narrow-gauge engines from the West Cornwall Railway. *Una* was numbered 2147 by the Great Western in 1876 and was withdrawn in June 1886. Note that the engine is in South Devon lined green livery. *Ian Allan Library*

Right: The engine *Etna*, a 4-4-0ST with 5ft 3in driving wheels, was built by Rothwell & Co in 1864 for the Carmarthen & Cardigan Railway. It was sold to the South Devon company in December 1868 and is pictured here at Newton Abbot in around 1870. *The late J. B. N. Ashford/by courtesy of A. Kingdom*

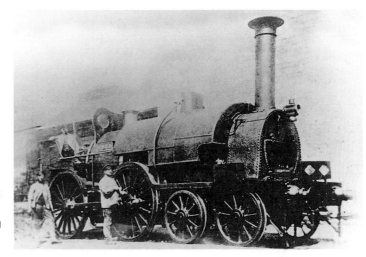

Below: Etna was taken over by the Great Western and numbered 2132, and is seen here in its later modified form with the nameplate removed. Note the hinged stop block in the foreground. *GWT Collection*

Right: Argo was one of eight goods engines supplied by Slaughter, Gruning between 1860 and 1864. All were 0-6-0 saddle tanks with inside frames; the first two were fitted with 4ft 6in wheels. *Argo*, which had 4ft 9in wheels, was delivered in October 1863. Numbered 2151 by the Great Western, it was withdrawn in May 1892. *Ian Allan/Bucknall Collection*

To work the new services, the South Devon purchased a further 47 engines over a nine-year period, 34 new and 13 secondhand. The new engines comprised six 4-4-0ST passenger engines and two 0-6-0ST goods engines: all were built by the Avonside Engine Co at Bristol and delivered during 1866. The 4-4-0s, although similar in design, differed from the earlier 4-4-0 engines in having inside plate frames.

Between 1868 and 1872, 13 secondhand tank engines were purchased from a variety of sources (five 4-4-0s, six 0-6-0s and two 2-4-0s). Also added to stock were four small tank engines: in 1869, *Taurus*, an 0-6-0ST built by Avonside; in 1871, the same company supplied *King*, a 2-4-0 side tank; the same year, the Ince Forge Company supplied *Prince*,

a 2-4-0ST. But probably the most interesting was the vertical-boilered well tank *Tiny*, built in 1868 for use on the Sutton Harbour branch. It was withdrawn from service in 1883, but saw subsequent use as a stationary boiler at Newton Abbot works, until 1927 when it was preserved by the Great Western and placed on public view on the down platform at Newton Abbot station. The only original broad-gauge engine to survive, it is currently on show in the South Devon Railway Museum at Buckfastleigh.

The final 22 engines ordered by the company were all new. Again built for the company by Avonside of Bristol between 1872 and 1875, these too were all tanks. They comprised four 4-4-0 passenger engines (similar in design to the 1866

Left: The 0-6-0ST *Redruth* was built by the West Cornwall Railway at its Carn Brea works in 1865, possibly from a kit of parts supplied by Slaughter, Gruning & Co. Constructed as a narrow-gauge 0-6-0 tender engine, it was purchased by the South Devon Railway in December 1871 and converted to an 0-6-0ST at Newton works. The photo shows the engine in its later state, converted with its wheels outside the frames and carrying its Great Western number 2156. It apparently spent most of its life shunting at Plymouth Millbay Goods, and was withdrawn from service in June 1887. *GWT Collection*

Left: *Zebra* was purchased from the Avonside Engine Co in October 1866 and was the last in a batch of six 4-4-0ST passenger engines with 5ft 8in coupled wheels. Supplied to the SDR by Avonside during 1866, they were the first to be constructed with inside plate frames. The engine is probably photographed as built, with an open cab. *GWT Collection*

Above: No 2125 *Sol* was delivered in November 1866, one of the engines built to Gooch's design specially for the heavy gradients on the South Devon Railway. The class was built with inside plate frames. This view shows the engine in its final Great Western condition. *Sol* was withdrawn in May 1892.
Ian Allan/Bucknall Collection

batch), 10 0-6-0 goods, and eight small-wheeled shunting engines. In anticipation of the demise of the broad gauge, they were designed to be easily converted to narrow gauge. In fact only nine of the goods engines and seven of the shunters were actually converted.

On 1 August 1876 the South Devon Railway ceased to exist as a separate company and was amalgamated into the Great Western. The 85 surviving South Devon Railway locomotives, which were all named, comprised nine 0-4-0Ts, three 2-4-0Ts, 40 4-4-0Ts, and 33 0-6-0Ts. They were taken into Great Western stock and numbered 2096-180.

The ex-South Devon Railway accident reports make interesting reading, and some in retrospect are actually quite amusing. One accident took place on 25 December 1883 about one mile south of Newton Abbot station. As the Christmas traffic was heavy, the Down mail train from London to Plymouth had been divided into two parts. The first portion, comprising an engine, a brake van and six coaches, reached Newton Abbot at 3.24am on the 25th. The engine and the last coach were detached, and the remaining portion, consisting of a brake van and five coaches, was to be sent on to Rattery with two engines, as there are steep rising gradients for the first 13 or 14 miles after leaving Newton Abbot. While the train was standing in the station, the pilot engine, a six-wheeled coupled tank, was attached to the front of the train. After coupling up the pilot, the porter went to the back of the train to detach the last coach which was to be left at Newton Abbott. He was not aware that a second engine was to be attached to the train.

The second engine, No 2122, backed onto the train just as the porter left. It was not coupled up, and at 3.35am the guard gave the signal for the train to depart. Both engine drivers sounded their steam whistles and the train left. There was thick fog at the time, and as the driver of the leading engine left the cutting south of the station he thought he was running faster than usual. Looking round, he found that his engine had no train attached to it. Because he could neither hear nor see his train, he assumed that he had left it at Newton Abbot and promptly slowed right down. Almost immediately the Down mail, which had picked up speed and was now running at about 30mph, collided with the engine. Both engines were badly damaged, but luckily just three passengers and both footplate crews were only slightly hurt.

Top: No 2159 *Saunders* started life as a Metropolitan condensing side tank. Built by the Great Western at Swindon in September 1866, it was sold to the South Devon Railway, and altered to a short saddle tank in July 1872. Re-acquired by the Great Western in 1876, it became a member of the 'Sir Watkin' class. It was again rebuilt, with a long saddle tank as seen in this picture. Note the mixed-gauge buffers.
Ian Allan/Bucknall Collection

Above: The first broad-gauge train, after arrival at Redruth in Cornwall in November 1866. It is hauled by the engine *Lance*, one of the first engines to be delivered to the South Devon Railway. Built by Longridge & Co in September 1851, *Lance* was first sent from Bedlington to Gloucester for trials on the Cheltenham line prior to being delivered to the South Devon. It was unfortunately terminally damaged during a collision near Menheniot on 2 December 1873 and was subsequently withdrawn. *The late J. B. N. Ashford/by courtesy of A. Kingdom*

Above: Romulus (No 2155) was one of two 0-6-0ST goods engines with 4ft 9in driving wheels that were constructed by the Avonside Engine Co in December 1866. The other was *Remus*, which was withdrawn in December 1886, but *Romulus*, shown here in GW ownership and still fitted with a small weatherboard cab, continued in service until the end of the broad gauge in May 1892. *GWT Collection*

Right: The aptly named 0-4-0 *Tiny* was probably the smallest engine ever to have run on the broad gauge. Built by Sara & Co of Plymouth in January 1868, it had a vertical boiler and 4ft 0in coupled wheels. *Tiny* was purchased by the SDR to replace horse traction on the Sutton Harbour branch. In its latter days it was used for shunting in Newton Abbot yard, and in June 1883 it was withdrawn and installed as a stationary boiler at Newton Abbot works, as pictured here. Interestingly, the works continued to be known as the South Devon works until about 1903. In 1927, *Tiny* was restored and placed on view on the down platform at Newton Abbot. *GWT Collection*

Below right: Stag was one of the final batch of 22 goods and passenger locomotives built for the South Devon Railway by the Avonside Engine Co between 1872 and 1875. *Stag* was delivered in December 1872, a 4-4-0ST with 5ft 9in coupled wheels, partially enclosed by the splashers. Numbered 2129 by the Great Western, *Stag* was withdrawn in May 1892, but together with fellow class member *Leopard* was used for shunting redundant broad-gauge stock at Swindon until June 1893. *GWT Collection*

Left: Vulcan was built for the South Devon Railway by the Avonside Engine Co in March 1874. Used mainly for goods work, it was taken over and renumbered 2169 by the Great Western, and is seen on the turntable at Falmouth around 1890. It ceased work in May 1892, and in April 1893 was converted to standard gauge and renumbered 1319, being finally withdrawn in June 1903. These small turntables were provided at locations where only tank engines were used. *GWT Collection*

Left: South Devon Railway 4-4-0ST *Osiris*, built by the Avonside Engine Co at Bristol in March 1875 and taken into Great Western stock as No 2131. This engine replaced the original *Osiris* which was built in April 1853, withdrawn in August 1873, and used at Portreath as a stationary engine for the incline. These later 5ft 9in-wheeled tanks were designed to be easily converted to run on the narrow gauge. *Osiris* and sister engine *Lance* differed from others in the class in having open splashers above the driving wheels and slightly larger 4ft 6in diameter boilers. *Osiris* was withdrawn from service on 20 May 1892. *Ian Allan Library*

Left: Between 1873 and 1875 the South Devon took delivery of eight small 0-4-0 tank engines. One of these was *Owl*, an 0-4-0 well tank built in January 1873 by the Avonside Engine Co for use in and around Plymouth docks. Taken over and numbered 2172 by the Great Western, it was withdrawn in June 1889 and subsequently sold to Pearson & Son for quarry use. Repurchased by the Great Western in June 1893, *Owl* was converted to standard gauge in August of the same year, and renumbered 1327. It was finally withdrawn from service in April 1913. *GWT Collection*

Right: Constructed in February 1875, *Jay* (No 2179) was an 0-4-0ST with outside cylinders and 3ft 0in coupled wheels. Used mainly for dock shunting in the Plymouth area, it is pictured here at Newton Abbot works, minus its connecting rods. Withdrawn in May 1892, it was converted to standard gauge and numbered 1333. *GWT Collection*

Centre right: This view shows the ex-SDR 2-4-0ST *Prince* at Brixham in around 1890. The engine which had 4ft coupled driving wheels, was built by the Ince Forge Co in June 1871. Numbered 2137 by the GWR, it was withdrawn on 20 May 1892 and converted to narrow gauge. It was renumbered 1316 in June 1893, and after withdrawal in May 1899 it apparently spent the next 36 years in use as a stationary boiler. *Ian Allan Library*

Below: Ex-South Devon Railway 4-4-0ST No 2128 *Leopard* derailed at Stray Park, Camborne, during a heavy snowstorm in the winter of 1891. *Leopard* was built by the Avonside Engine Co for the SDR in December 1872. Taken over by the Great Western in February 1876 and numbered 2128, it was withdrawn from service in May 1892 and used for the next year shunting withdrawn broad-gauge stock at Swindon. *Leopard* was cut up in June 1893. Note the loco jack alongside the smokebox. *GWT Collection*

Above: The Torbay & Brixham Railway had just two engines. The longest serving engine, *Queen*, was built in 1852 by E. B. Wilson as a contractor's engine for use on the construction of the Portland breakwater. It was one of several 0-4-0 well tanks with inside sandwich frames and 4ft driving wheels built by the company for this purpose. *Queen* was purchased by the Torbay & Brixham Railway in 1868 and then mortgaged to the South Devon Railway in July 1870. This diminutive engine continued to work on the Torbay & Brixham until it was withdrawn from service on 1 January 1883. *Ian Allan/Bucknall Collection*

Below: In January 1877 the Great Western sold the ex-South Devon 0-4-0ST *Raven* to the Torbay & Brixham Co to supplement *Queen*. Built by Avonside in November 1874 with 3ft driving wheels, *Raven* was numbered 2175 when the company was taken over by the Great Western on 1 January 1883. It was converted to standard gauge and fitted with a new boiler in August 1892, and renumbered 1329. It was sold to the Wantage Tramway in March 1910, but was cut up at Wantage, after a long period out of use, in around 1930. *Ian Allan Library*